French Bulldog

French Bulldog Care & Information Guide

French BullDog Characteristics, Personality and Temperament, Diet, Health, Where to Buy, Cost, Rescue and Adoption, Care and Grooming, Training, Breeding, and Much More Included!

By Lolly Brown

Foreword

The French Bulldog is among the top 10 most famous breeds of dogs. They have a unique charm that captivates a lot of people. With a squashed-looking face, round eyes, and adorable bat ears, you're bound to find it hard to resist their charisma. Maybe that's why it's also a very popular breed among celebrities. Leonardo DiCaprio, Hugh Jackman and Lady Gaga, to name a few, all own this very lovable and ugly but cute dog.

If you're interested in getting a French Bulldog as a pet, it would be prudent to educate yourself on the breed as much as you can so you can make an informed decision on whether this breed is the right match for you or not. As it happens, you're in luck because the book you are currently reading contains all the important information you'll need about French Bulldogs so go on and turn the page!

Table of Contents

Introduction

Bringing a dog home is a big responsibility and that responsibility begins when you're choosing the right breed for you. Choosing the right breed is like choosing a life partner because you're making a commitment and compatibility plays a big role. It's even more literal for dogs because they are the most loyal creatures in the world and they will live their entire lives as your companion. Ain't it a shame that they have shorter life spans than humans? So make the right choice because they deserve a good home where they will be loved and happy.

This book is all about French Bulldogs and basically contains all the important things you need to know when considering bringing one home as a pet.

Introduction

When you hear the words French Bulldog, your mind probably conjures an image of a small but sturdy dog with a flat face and bat ears. Their appearance is very distinct, unforgettable and endearing. If you're looking for a companion, you can't go wrong with this breed. They are very loving and affectionate. Also, they are born to be entertainers and comedians so you are guaranteed an endless supply of laughter. Your home will be a happy place if you decide to keep one around. These are just a few of the things that people love about this breed. But of course, there are also cons to owning a French Bulldog.

Before even considering purchasing a French Bulldog, it would be smart to educate yourself first on what it really takes to be a dog owner and, specifically, to own a French Bulldog. To learn more about this wonderful breed and what it entails to keep one as a pet, please do read on.

Glossary of Dog Terms

AKC – American Kennel Club, the largest purebred dog registry in the United States

Bat Ears – Erect ears with the orifice facing front, broad at the base elongating to a round tip

Breed – A domestic race of dogs having a common gene pool and characterized appearance/function

Breed Standard – A published document describing the look, movement, and behavior of the perfect specimen of a particular breed

Brindle - oat that is predominantly a dark color with lighter colored hairs mixed in

Coat – The hair covering of a dog; some breeds have two coats, and outer coat and undercoat; also known as a double coat. Examples of breeds with double coats include German Shepherd, Siberian Husky, Akita, etc.

Condition – The health of the dog as shown by its skin, coat, behavior, and general appearance

Crate – A container used to house and transport dogs; also called a cage or kennel

Fawn – Light tan color

Flatulence – Gassiness

Groom – To brush, trim, comb or otherwise make a dog's coat neat in appearance

Kennel – A building or enclosure where dogs are kept

Litter – A group of puppies born at one time

Liver – Brown

Mate – To breed a male and female dog

Mouse – blue

Neuter – To castrate a male dog or spay a female dog

Pedigree – The written record of a dog's genealogy going back three generations or more

Puppy – A dog under 12 months of age

Purebred – A dog whose sire and dam belong to the same breed and who are of unmixed descent

Shedding – The natural process whereby old hair falls off the dog's body as it is replaced by new hair growth.

Smooth Coat – Short hair that is close-lying

Spay – The surgery to remove a female dog's ovaries, rendering her incapable of breeding

Styptic powder – Remedy to stop bleeding

Trim – To groom a dog's coat by plucking or clipping

Wean – The process through which puppies transition from subsisting on their mother's milk to eating solid food

Whelping – The act of birthing a litter of puppies

Introduction

Chapter One: Understanding French Bulldogs

French Bulldogs make delightful pets if you are compatible with them. They are funny and loads of fun to have around. If you are fascinated by this breed, then you should take the time to learn everything you can about them. In this chapter you will find an overview of the French Bulldog including their history, physical characteristics and more. This knowledge will help you understand these dogs better, and by the end of the chapter hopefully you would have formed an inclination as to whether this breed is suitable for you or not.

Facts About French Bulldogs

If the French Bulldog were to be described in one word, the word would probably be 'lovable'. These dogs possess a lot of traits that most people would want in a pet, which makes them very easy to love and makes it easier to overlook, or at least tolerate, their flaws and faults. They fall under the breed group of companions, and they are the type that seeks constant love and affection from their owners. However, if overindulged, they may become territorial and easily jealous which may develop hostile behavior towards other pets or family members. These dogs are usually hilarious, well-behaved with just the right amount of playfulness, and adaptable. They are laid back and generally easy to please. Simply lying down on your lap is enough to satisfy them and make them happy.

In terms of size, their height ranges from 11 – 13 inches and the average weight for the breed is between 22 – 28 pounds. They have short and smooth coats, but unlike other breeds with similar coats, they don't shed a lot. Their skin is loose and wrinkled in the head and shoulders. The French Bulldog comes with a wide array of colors and patterns such as brindle, fawn, white, black, shades of gray, blue, cream, chocolate, and pied patterns. However, not all colors are acceptable by the AKC breed standard for show dogs. The French Bulldog is small, compact and stocky with an alert stance.

One of the challenges that come with the French Bulldog breed is training. If you want to enjoy your dog to its maximum potential, you will want him to be well-mannered and respectful. Therefore, you will need to be fully loaded with patience when you train him. Sooner rather than later, you will find out that this breed carries the unfortunate gene of stubbornness. When left unchecked, they can become manipulative and no one wants that.

French Bulldogs don't bark often and without good reason. So when they do bark, immediately search for what he's trying to call your attention to. These dogs are generally quiet but sometimes they can be talkative and make indescribable sounds akin to speaking gibberish or out-of-this-world noises. Owners of French Bulldogs have mixed feelings about the famous Frenchie Death Yodel, but it's definitely something to watch out for. It kind of sounds like high-pitched squeaking. If you want a preview, there are a lot of videos on YouTube that you can check out.

French Bulldogs make dependable guard dogs because they are attentive and effective in alerting their owners due to their barking philosophy. Their attachment to their person or family runs very deep, which makes them very protective to the point that they would die to save them if the need ever arises.

Their lifespan usually ranges between 8 – 14 years. Unfortunately, the genetic makeup of this breed is just a little short of catastrophic which is the reason why French Bulldogs come with a myriad of existing and potential health concerns and problems. This particular subject will be discussed all throughout the book.

Summary of French Bulldogs Facts

Pedigree: exact origin unknown, debatable between England and France

AKC Group: Companion, Non-sporting

Breed Size: small and stocky

Height: average 12 inches

Weight: 22 – 28 pounds

Coat Length: short

Coat Texture: fine and smooth

Shedding: minimal

Color: brindle, fawn, white, brindle and white, black, mouse, cream, chocolate, gray

Eyes: dark in color, lighter in light colored coats – no white showing when looking forward

Nose: black

Ears: bat ears

Tail: short, hung low, straight or screwed

Temperament: clownish, affectionate, well-behaved, easygoing, playful, alert

Strangers: generally friendly to everyone

Children: generally good with children, but (like all dogs) should be supervised around young and small children

Other Dogs: generally good with other dogs and other animals if properly trained and socialized

Training: difficult due to short attention span and stubbornness

Exercise Needs: minimal exercise needed, daily 15-minute walks are sufficient

Health Conditions: respiratory disorders, joint diseases, blood disease, spinal disorders, skin sensitivities

Lifespan: 8 to 14 years

Nickname: Frenchie

French Bulldog Breed History

The history of the French Bulldogs has become muddled over time. Some accounts claim that toy bulldogs were crossbred with terriers and pugs in England while some accounts claim that the crossbreeding happened in France. What remains to be constant is that toy bulldogs were all the rage among lace makers in the 19th century at England, wherein the dogs were used as lap warmers. When the lace industry was displaced to France, the workers brought their dogs with them and that's when their numbers grew and their popularity rose which led to the acknowledgement of the breed. It was named

Bouledogue Francais which is just the translation of French Bulldog in French.

Chapter Two: Things to Know Before Getting a French Bulldog

Have you already fallen in love with the lovable and irresistible French Bulldog? Not so fast. Before you get ahead of yourself, there is still the matter of the practical aspects of owning a dog. It's not all fun and cuddles: owning dogs cost a lot. In this chapter you will find out just how much damage they can do to your bank account plus other practical material you need to know before embarking on the journey of being a dog owner. This chapter should help you further in making an educated decision on whether you are capable and ready to own a pet.

Do You Need a License?

Before purchasing a French Bulldog, you should learn about local licensing requirements that may affect you. The licensing requirements for dog owners vary from one country to another so you may need to do a little bit of research on your own to determine whether you need a dog license or not. In the United States, there are no federal requirements for dog licensing – it is determined at the state level. While some states do not, most states require dog owners to license their dogs on an annual basis.

When you apply for a dog license you will have to submit proof that your dog has been given a rabies vaccine. Dog licenses in the United States cost about $25 (£16.25) per year and they can be renewed annually when you renew your dog's rabies vaccine. Even if your state doesn't require you to license your dog it is still a good idea because it will help someone to identify him if he gets lost so they can return him to you.

In the United Kingdom, licensing requirements for dog owners are a little bit different. The U.K. requires that all dog owners license their dogs and the license can be renewed every twelve months. The cost to license your dog in the U.K. is similar to the U.S. but you do not have to have your dog vaccinated against rabies. In fact, rabies does not exist in the U.K. because it was eradicated through careful control measures. If you travel with your dog to or from the U.K., you will have to obtain a special animal moving license and your dog may have to undergo a period of quarantine to make sure he doesn't carry disease into the country.

Do French Bulldogs Get Along with Other Pets?

If a French Bulldog is successfully trained and adequately socialized, he is generally very friendly towards all kinds of animals and he gets along well with other pets. However, if spoiled too much by their person, they become territorial and jealous of other pets going near or getting any attention from their person.

How Many French Bulldogs Should You Keep?

There is an upside and a downside to keeping more than one French Bulldog and it will be up to you to decide which one weighs more for you. The upside of having more than one French Bulldog is having no shortage of entertainment and affection. And the downside is the chance of dealing with quarreling for attention amongst themselves. Remember: these dogs thrive on being the center of attention and jealousy can become a problem.

However, there is a belief that if the breed is the right match for you, then you'll most likely desire another one or more. If you do decide to get more than one, make sure you don't play favorites because it might cause emotional damage to the less favored one/s.

How Much Does it Cost to Keep a French Bulldog?

Most people who aspire to own a dog don't realize that the cost is more than just the purchase price itself. Owning pets mean including them in your budget because the expenses are as a regular as your grocery and utility bills. Spending on your French Bulldog will begin even before you take him home because you have to prepare for his arrival and you have to purchase a crate, toys, indoor gates or fences, and food bowls. And one source says that this breed ranks ninth in the most expensive cost for medical expenses. The responsibility of being a dog owner also includes being able to provide for their needs so before you take one home make sure that you can keep up with the expenses. In this section you will receive an overview of the initial costs and monthly costs to keep a French Bulldog.

Initial Costs

The initial costs for keeping a French Bulldog include those costs that you must cover before you can bring your dog home. Some of the initial costs you will need to cover include your dog's crate, food/water bowls, toys and accessories, microchipping, initial vaccinations, spay/neuter surgery and supplies for grooming and nail clipping – it also includes the cost of the dog itself.

You will find an overview of each of these costs as well as an estimate for each cost below:

Purchase Price–The cost to purchase a French Bulldog can vary greatly depending where you find the dog. You can adopt a rescue French Bulldog for as little as $175 (£158) but purchasing a puppy, especially a purebred puppy from an AKC-registered breeder, could be much more costly. The average cost for a French Bulldog is $2,050 (£1,845). Just be cautious when buying from unregistered breeders and do a background check on their credibility. Make sure the puppy is completely healthy.

Crate–The French Bulldog is a small breed and will stay that way even if he's an adult already so you'll be able to save money that would otherwise be needed to buy a bigger one. The average cost for a small dog crate is about $30 (£19.50) in most cases.

Indoor Fences/Gates – Aside from the crate, you'll need to create a space for your puppy that he can acknowledge as his own where you will set up his bed and toys. The average cost for these fences/gates is $100 (£70).

Orthopedic Bed–It is ideal to teach your puppy early on that there is a designated place for him to sleep. And you want your Frenchie to be as comfortable as possible so an orthopedic bed is highly recommended since they experience joint discomfort and pain sometimes. The ideal orthopedic bed costs $42 (£38).

Food/Water Bowls – In addition to providing your dog with a crate to sleep in, you should also make sure he has a set of high-quality food and water bowls. The best materials for these are stainless steel because it is easy to clean and doesn't harbor bacteria. Choose bowls that are heavy so that the dog won't be able to push or tip it over and make a mess. The average cost for a quality set of stainless steel bowls is about $20 (£18).

Toys–Giving your French Bulldog plenty of toys to play with will help to keep him from chewing on things that are not toys – they can also be used to provide mental stimulation and enrichment. To start out, plan to buy an assortment of toys for your dog until you learn what kind he prefers. You may want to budget a cost of $50 (£45) for toys just to be sure you have enough to last through the puppy phase.

Microchipping – In the United States and United Kingdom there are no federal or state requirements saying that you have to have your dog microchipped, but it is a very good idea. Your French Bulldog could slip out of his harness on a walk or lose his ID tag. If someone finds him without identification, they can take him to a shelter to have his microchip scanned. A microchip is something that is implanted under your dog's skin and it carries a number that is linked to your contact information. The procedure takes just a few minutes to perform and it only costs about $30 (£19.50) in most cases.

Initial Vaccinations – During your dog's first year of life, he will require a number of different vaccinations. If you purchase your puppy from a reputable breeder, he might already have had a few but you'll still need more over the next few months as well as booster shots each year. You should budget about $50 (£32.50) for initial vaccinations just to be prepared.

Spay/Neuter Surgery – If you don't plan to breed your bulldog you should have him or her neutered or spayed before 6 months of age. The cost for this surgery will vary depending where you go and on the sex of your dog. If you go to a traditional veterinary surgeon, the cost for spay/neuter surgery could be very high but you can save money by going to a veterinary clinic. The average cost for neuter surgery is $50 to $100 (£32.50 - £65) and spay surgery costs about $100 to $200 (£65 - £130).

Supplies/Accessories – In addition to purchasing your bulldog's crate and food/water bowls, you should also purchase some basic grooming supplies as well as a leash and harness. The cost for these items will vary depending on the quality, but you should budget about $100 (£32.50) for these extra costs.

Initial Costs for French Bulldogs		
Cost	One Dog	Two Dogs
Purchase Price	$175 - $2,050 (£158 - £1,845)	$350 - $4,100 (£315 - £3,690)
Crate	$30 (£19.50)	$60 (£39)
Fences/Gates	$100 (£70)	$100 (£70)
Orthopedic Bed	$42 (£38)	$84 (£76)
Food/Water Bowl	$20 (£18)	$40 (£36)
Toys	$50 (£45)	$100 (£90)
Microchipping	$30 (£19.50)	$60 (£39)
Vaccinations	$50 (£32.50)	$100 (£65)
Spay/Neuter	$50 to $200 (£32.50 - £130)	$100 to $400 (£65 - £260)
Accessories	$100 (£90)	$100 (£90)
Total	$602 to $2,672 (£542 - £2,405)	$1,094 to $5144 (£945 – £4,630)

*Costs may vary depending on location
**U.K. prices based on an estimated exchange of $1 = £0.90

Monthly Costs

The monthly costs for keeping a French Bulldog as a pet include those costs which recur on a monthly basis. The most important monthly cost for keeping a dog is, of course, food. In addition to food, however, you'll also need to think about things like annual license renewal, toy replacements, and veterinary exams. <u>You will find an overview of each of these costs as well as an estimate for each cost on below</u>:

Food and Treats – Feeding your French Bulldog a healthy diet is very important for his health and wellness. A high-quality diet for dogs is not cheap, so you should be prepared to spend around $54 (£49) on a large bag of high-quality dog food which will last you at least a month. You should also include a monthly budget of about $10 (£6.50) for treats.

License Renewal – The cost to license your French Bulldog will generally be about $25 (£16.25) and you can renew the license for the same price each year. License renewal cost divided over 12 months is about $2 (£1.30) per month.

Veterinary Exams – In order to keep your French Bulldog healthy you should take him to the veterinarian about every six months after he passes puppyhood. You might have to take him more often for the first 12 months to make sure he gets his vaccines on time. The average cost for a vet visit is about $40 (£26) so, if you have two visits per year, it averages to about $7 (£4.55) per month. However, depending on how healthy or unhealthy your dog is, this amount is relative to the medical care he will need.

Other Costs – In addition to the monthly costs for your bulldog's food, license renewal, and vet visits there are also some other cost you might have to pay occasionally. These costs might include things like replacements for worn-out toys, a larger harness as your puppy grows, cleaning products, and more. You should budget about $15 (£9.75) per month for extra costs.

Monthly Costs for French Bulldogs		
Cost	One Dog	Two Dogs
Food and Treats	$64 (£55.50)	$128 (£115)
License Renewal	$2 (£1.30)	$4 (£3.60)
Veterinary Exams	$7 (£4.55)	$14 (£12.60)
Other Costs	$15 (£9.75)	$30 (£19.50)
Total	$118 (£107)	$236(£212)

*Costs may vary depending on location
**U.K. prices based on an estimated exchange of $1 = £0.90

What are the Pros and Cons of French Bulldog?

Part of the French Bulldog's charm is its deformed face. Rather than repulse people, it has the opposite effect (for most people anyway). So if you're one of those people who has fallen for the charm of the French Bulldog, it would be wise to get to know more about having them as a pet and the best way to help you decide is to learn the good and the bad about them. You will find a list of pros and cons for the French Bulldog breed listed on the following page:

Pros for the French Bulldog Breed

- Naturally amusing and entertainers – you will never get bored when you have them around
- Great watch dogs because of their alertness
- Generally friendly with everyone they meet
- Affectionate and loving – great companions
- Does not bark excessively
- Adaptable
- Suited for apartment living
- Easy to groom so you don't have to spend for it
- Doesn't need much exercise
- Not fussy – calm and easygoing
- Small but durable – easy to take anywhere and no need to worry too much about getting easily hurt
- Generally likes to keep themselves clean

Cons for the French Bulldog Breed

- Serious health issues
- Does not do well when left alone, needs constant attention, suffers from separation anxiety
- Has a tendency to become (too) clingy
- Stubborn, sometimes manipulative – needs special training that would be difficult for novice dog owners
- Not suited for warm and humid weather, needs air-conditioning
- Must tolerate wheezing, snorting, snoring, slobbering and gassiness
- Acquires doggy odor if not bathed regularly
- In summary, more expensive and high maintenance than other breeds in several aspects

Chapter Three: Purchasing French Bulldogs

If you've already made up your mind about getting a French Bulldog, then congratulations to you. You have approximately ten to twelve years of fun and laughter, love and affection, with a sprinkling of grumbles and troublesomeness here and there. But where to start looking for your dog? Should you go to a pet store? Should you shop online? Read on to find the answers to your questions. In this chapter, you will also receive valuable tips for picking out a healthy Frenchie puppy and puppy-proofing your home.

Where Can You Buy French Bulldogs?

When you've made a decision to become a dog owner, the fun begins as soon as you start hunting for the dog that will win your heart and make you want to take him home.

Many people think that the best place to find a dog is at the pet store but, unfortunately, they are greatly mistaken. While the puppies at the pet store might look cute and cuddly, there is no way to know whether they are actually healthy or well-bred. Many pet stores get their puppies from puppy mills and they sell the puppies to unsuspecting dog lovers. Puppy mill puppies are often already sick by the time they make it to the pet store, often traveling across state lines to get there.

A puppy mill is a type of breeding facility that focuses on breeding and profit more than the health and wellbeing of the dogs. Puppy mills usually keep their dogs in squalid conditions, forcing them to bear litter after litter of puppies with little to no rest in between. Many of the breeders used in puppy mills are poorly bred themselves or unhealthy to begin with which just ensures that the puppies will have the same problems. The only time you should bring home a puppy from a pet store is if the store has a partnership with a local shelter and that is where they get their dogs. If the pet store can't tell you which breeder the puppies came from, or if they don't offer you any paperwork or registration for the puppy, it is likely that the puppy came from a puppy mill.

Rather than purchasing a puppy from a pet store, your best bet is to find a reputable French Bulldog breeder – preferably and AKC-registered breeder in the United States or a Kennel Club-registered breeder in the U.K. If you visit the website for either of these organizations you can find a list of breeders for all of the club-recognized breeds. You can also look for breeders on the website for other breed clubs like The French Bull Dog Club of America or The French Bulldog Club of England. Even if these organizations don't provide a list of breeders you may be able to speak with members to find out more.

If you don't have your heart set on a puppy, you may consider adopting a rescue from a local shelter. There are many benefits associated with rescuing an adult dog. For one thing, adoption fees are generally under $200 (£180) which is much more affordable than the $800 to $1,200 (£720 to £1,080) fee to buy a puppy from a breeder. Plus, an adult dog will already be housetrained. As an added bonus, most shelters spay/neuter their dogs before adopting them out so you won't have to pay for the surgery yourself. Another benefit is that an adult dog has already surpassed the puppy stage so his personality is set – with a puppy you can never quite be sure how your puppy will turn out.

If you are thinking about adopting a French Bulldog, consider one of these breed-specific rescues:

United States Rescues:

French Bulldog Rescue Network
<http://www.frenchbulldogrescue.org/>

Chicago French Bulldog Rescue
<http://www.frenchieporvous.org/>

French Bulldog Village
<http://frenchbulldogvillage.net/>

Short Noses Only Rescue Team
<http://www.snortrescue.org/>

French Bulldog Last Chance Rescue
<http://frenchbulldoglastchance.org/>

United Kingdom Rescues:

French Bulldog Rescue GB

<http://www.frenchbulldogrescuegb.co.uk/>

French Bulldog Breed Rescue

<http://www.thekennelclub.org.uk/services/public/findare
scue/Default.aspx?breed=4088>

Bring Joy, Adopt a Dog

<http://www.dogsblog.com/category/french-bulldog/>

French Bulldogs Needing Homes

<http://www.preloved.co.uk/adverts/list/3359/dogs.html?k
eyword=french+bulldogs+needing+homes>

How to Choose a Reputable French Bulldog Breeder

When you are ready to start looking for a French Bulldog puppy you may begin your search for a breeder online. A simple internet search will probably give you a variety of results but, if you want to find a reputable breeder, you may have to dig a little deeper. The French Bull Dog Club of America and The French Bulldog Club of England are great places to start. Compile a list of breeders from whatever sources you can and then take the time to go through each option to determine whether the breeder is reputable and responsible or not. You do not want to run the risk of purchasing a puppy from a hobby breeder or from someone who doesn't follow responsible breeding practices. If you aren't careful about where you get your puppy, you could end up with a puppy that is already sick.

Once you have your list of breeders on hand you can go through them one-by-one to narrow down your options. Go through the following steps to do so:

- Visit the website for each breeder on your list (if they have one) and look for key points about the breeder's history and experience.
  - o Check for club registrations and a license, if applicable.
  - o If the website doesn't provide any information about the facilities or the breeder you are best just moving on.
- After ruling out some of the breeders, contact the remaining breeders on your list by phone
  - o Ask the breeder the following questions:
    - How old are the parents?
    - Can you provide me with the health clearances of the parents?
    - Why did you decide upon this particular breeding?
    - Can you tell me about the dogs in the 3 generation pedigree?
    - How did you raise the puppies? Have you started training and socializing?

- Can you provide references from previous buyers?
  - The answers to these questions must be along these lines:
    - The female dog must not be younger than 18 months and the male should not be younger than 12 months. Dogs must be given time to mature before being bred.
    - The breeder must be able to present you with a Canine Health Information Center number as an assurance that the parents were screened and deemed healthy and fit to be bred.
    - The answer should have been well-thought out and it should include a rational objective.
    - A good breeder will be able to give you a detailed account of the 3 generation pedigree without batting an eyelash because he knows it by heart and he is proud of it.
    - The breeder should have already started introducing the world to the puppy and should be able to teach you how to continue training and socialization.

- A good breeder stays in touch with the owners to provide assistance so he should be able to give you references.
  - Expect a reputable breeder to ask you questions about yourself as well – a responsible breeder wants to make sure that his puppies go to good homes.
- Schedule an appointment to visit the facilities for the remaining breeders on your list after you've weeded a few more of them out.
  - Ask for a tour of the facilities, including the place where the breeding stock is kept as well as the facilities housing the puppies.
  - If things look unorganized or unclean, do not purchase from the breeder.
  - Make sure the breeding stock is in good condition and that the puppies are all healthy-looking and active.
- Narrow down your list to a final few options and then interact with the puppies to make your decision.
  - Make sure the breeder provides some kind of health guarantee and ask about any vaccinations the puppies may have already received.
- Put down a deposit, if needed, to reserve a puppy if they aren't ready to come home yet.

Tips for Selecting a Healthy French Bulldog Puppy

After you have narrowed down your options for breeders you then need to pick out your puppy. If you are a first-time dog owner, do not let yourself become caught up in the excitement of a new puppy – take the time to make a careful selection. If you rush the process you could end up with a puppy that isn't healthy or one whose personality isn't compatible with your family. <u>Follow the steps below to pick out your French Bulldog puppy</u>:

- Ask the breeder to give you a tour of the facilities, especially where the puppies are kept.
  - o Make sure the facilities where the puppies are housed are clean and sanitary – if there is evidence of diarrhea, do not purchase one of the puppies because they may already be sick.
- Take a few minutes to observe the litter as a whole, watching how the puppies interact with each other.
  - o The puppies should be active and playful, interacting with each other in a healthy way.
  - o Avoid puppies that appear to be lethargic and those that have difficulty moving – they are most probably sick.
- Approach the litter and watch how the puppies react to you when you do.

- o If the puppies appear frightened they may not be properly socialized and you do not want a puppy like that.
- o Some of the puppies may be somewhat cautious, but most of them should be very friendly, curious and interested in you.
- Let the puppies approach you and give them time to sniff and explore you before you interact with them.
  - o Pet the puppies and encourage them to play with a toy, taking the opportunity to observe their personalities.
  - o Single out any of the puppies that you think might be a good fit and spend a little time with them.
- Pick up the puppy and hold him to see how he responds to human contact.
  - o The puppy should be affectionate and playful. It shouldn't be frightened of you and it should enjoy being pet.
- Examine the puppy's body for signs of illness and injury
  - o The puppy should have clear, bright eyes with no discharge. The coat should be even, no patches of hair loss or discoloration.
  - o The ears should be bat ears, clean and clear with no discharge or inflammation.

- o The nose should be black. The only time lighter colored noses are acceptable is if the dog's color is lighter as well.
- o If you're entertaining the idea of entering your French Bulldog in shows, don't purchase the following colors: solid black, mouse, liver, black and tan, black and white. These are disqualifications for the breed standard.
- o The puppy's stomach may be round but it shouldn't be distended or swollen.
- o The puppy should be able to walk and run normally without any mobility problems.
- Narrow down your options and choose the puppy that you think is the best fit.

Once you've chosen your puppy, ask the breeder about the next steps. Do not take the puppy home if it isn't at least 9 or 10 weeks old because French Bulldogs may become petulant and nasty when separated from their mothers and their litter too soon. And of course you have to make sure that it has been fully weaned and is already eating solid food.

Puppy-Proofing Your Home

After you've picked out your puppy you may still have to wait a few weeks until you can bring him home. During this time you should take steps to prepare your home, making it a safe place for your puppy. The process of making your home safe for your puppy is called "puppy proofing" and it involves removing or storing away anything and everything that could harm your puppy. It might help for you to crawl around the house on your hands and knees, viewing things from your puppy's perspective to find potential threats.

On the following page you will find a list of things you should do when you are puppy-proofing your home:

- Make sure your trash and recycling containers have a tight-fitting lid or store them in a cabinet.

- Put away all open food containers and keep them out of reach of your puppy.

- Store cleaning products and other hazardous chemicals in a locked cabinet or pantry where your puppy can't get them.

- Make sure electrical cords and blind pulls are wrapped up and placed out of your puppy's reach.

- Pick up any small objects or toys that could be a choking hazard if your puppy chews on them.

- Cover or drain any open bodies of water such as the toilet, and outdoor pond, etc.

- Store any medications and beauty products in the medicine cabinet out of your puppy's reach.

- Check your home for any plants that might be toxic to dogs and remove them or put them out of reach.

- Block off fire places, windows, and doors so your puppy can't get into trouble.

- Close off any stairwells and block the entry to rooms where you do not want your puppy to be.

Chapter Four: Caring for French Bulldogs

After learning about the practical aspects of keeping a French Bulldog as a pet, you can now move on to learning how to care for your dog and the tasks involved. This section talks about his habitat and exercise requirements, and will teach you how to prepare your home and make it an ideal environment for your puppy. It is vital for both you and your puppy that he has a space to call his own so that you can feel safe knowing that you have a way to keep him confined in your absence without always keeping him in a crate.

Before bringing your French Bulldog home

You should ask yourself these questions first:

- **Do you spend most of your time away from home? If yes, will you be able to bring your dog along with you?**

  French Bulldogs don't like being alone or away from their owners for long periods of time and they suffer from separation anxiety. It'll be cruel to subject them to that if you're just planning on leaving them at home all the time.

- **Are you equipped to pay extra medical bills?**

  French Bulldogs are known to be high-maintenance in terms of medical conditions so you have to be sure that you can shell out money in case of emergencies.

- **Do you have what it takes to be a firm, consistent, patient and creative trainer?**

  These are all requirements for a well-behaved French Bulldog because they are very obstinate creatures and these qualities are needed in order to successfully train them.

- **Can you tolerate drool, annoying noises and occasional smelly odors?**

  This breed snores, snorts, wheezes, and farts regularly. You have been warned.

For families, it would also be a good idea to sit down and ask all members if they are all on board with getting a dog. Once the decision is agreed upon, you can all discuss house rules and the distribution of tasks when caring for the dog (e.g. off-limits areas, feeding time, potty time, etc.) However, you should assign only one member of the family who will be the primary authority figure of the dog and will be in charge of housebreaking and training at all times.

Habitat and Exercise Requirements for French Bulldogs

The beauty of owning a French Bulldog is not having to worry about your living space or your fitness regime (or lack thereof). These little, adorable creatures can adapt to apartments or big houses or anything in between. They don't need yards or vast spaces to feel at home. In fact, a significant percentage of this breed would probably be perfectly satisfied to lounge on just one couch with you for the rest of their life. Some of them enjoy playing but due to their size, they don't really need a lot of space to be able to play. Your living room would suffice or you can take them out for a short walk. When walking your dog, be sure to lead the way to establish your authority. To prevent obesity, they need daily exercise for about 15 minutes. To prevent respiratory problems, do not exceed the physical activities allowed by their low stamina and endurance. A sign that you should stop and let them rest is when they start panting. Furthermore, in relation to their respiratory health concerns, they are not suited to live in places that don't have air-conditioners to fight the heat of high-temperature days. Needless to say, they should be kept in cool places as much as possible. In case it is otherwise unavoidable, be sure to have cooling pads and drinking water for first aid. Don't take them out for exercise on warm or humid days and definitely do not leave them under the sun for a long time. When you plan to stay outside for a long time—under tolerable weather conditions for your pet—apply canine sunscreen on your dog because this breed gets sunburned and it's awfully painful for them. For owners that have a pool or who are fond of beach trips, it is of the utmost importance to know that your French Bulldog will instantly sink and drown in any body of water that exceeds their height. Constant supervision is a must when around dangerous-level waters. Fortunately for people who would insist on swimming with their Frenchies, there are life vests available for them.

Now, let's move on to how you can ensure that your dog feels at-home and is comfortable. First, you will need to provide him with certain things. A crate is one of the most important things you will need when you bring your new puppy home. Not only will it be a place for your puppy to sleep, but it will also be a place where you can confine him during the times when you are away from home or when you cannot keep a close eye on him. Your puppy will also need some other basic things like a water bowl, a food bowl, a harness, a leash, toys, and grooming supplies.

When shopping for food and water bowls, safety and sanitation are the top two considerations. Stainless steel is the best material to go with because it is easy to clean and resistant to bacteria. Ceramic is another good option. Heavy bowls are also a plus because the puppy will be unable to tip it over or push it across the floor which will save you from cleaning unnecessary mess. Avoid plastic food and water bowls because they can become scratched and the scratches may harbor bacteria. Remember that it is important to opt for a harness instead of a collar for this breed, and you should choose one that is appropriate to his size. This may mean that you will purchase several harnesses and leashes while your puppy is still growing. A harness will be helpful during leash training because it will improve your control over your puppy.

Provide your puppy with an assortment of different toys and let him figure out which ones he likes. Having a variety of toys around the house is very important because you'll need to use them to redirect your puppy's natural chewing behavior as he learns what he is and is not allowed to chew on. As for grooming supplies, you'll need a rubber hound glove or soft bristle brush for daily brushing.

Above all, what you need to remember is that the French Bulldog will thrive in a home where he is showered with attention and love.

Setting Up Your Puppy's Area

Before you bring your Frenchie puppy home, you should set up a particular area in your home for him to call his own. The ideal setup will include your puppy's crate, a comfy dog bed, his food and water bowls, an assortment of toys, and litter trays since this breed are indoor dogs. You can arrange all of these items in a small room that is easy to block off using indoor fences or gates, or you can use a puppy playpen to give your puppy some free space while still keeping him somewhat confined. It would be ideal to choose a room where most of the activity in the house happens so that your puppy won't feel isolated.

When you bring your puppy home you'll have to work with him a lot to get him used to the crate. It is very important that you do this because the last thing you want is your puppy to form a negative association with the crate. If this happens, it will be very difficult to make your puppy forget it and it will most likely ruin your success at house training. It is vital that your puppy learns that the crate is his own special place, a place where he can go to relax and take a nap if he wants to. If you use the crate as punishment, your puppy will not want to use it.

To get your puppy used to the crate, try tossing a few treats into it and let him go fish them out. Feeding your puppy his meals in the crate with the door open will be helpful as well. You can also incorporate the crate into your playtime, tossing toys into the crate or hiding treats under a blanket in the crate. As your puppy gets used to the crate you can start keeping him in it with the door closed for short periods of time, working your way up to longer periods. Just be sure to let your puppy outside before and after you confine him and never force him to stay in the crate for longer than he is physically capable of holding his bowels and his bladder.

Chapter Five: Meeting Your French Bulldog's Nutritional Needs

It has already been established in this book that French Bulldogs are high-maintenance dogs. Their nutritional needs and proper diet are not an exemption to that claim. These dogs are allergic to a lot of ingredients used in low-quality and cheap dog food so you should refrain from feeding those to your Frenchie. If you skimp on their food, you will only end up spending more on medications. In this chapter, you will be given basic guidelines on feeding your dog and specific high-quality brands that are the best recommendations for French Bulldogs.

The Nutritional Needs of French Bulldogs

French Bulldogs need high-quality dog food that specifically contains at least two sources of protein, carbohydrates from sweet potatoes and complex plants, and omega-rich fats. Their food should not contain corn, soy, and grain which are found in all cheap dog food brands so stay away from those if you want to maintain a healthy pet.

The breakdown of the French Bulldog's proper diet are as follows:

- 30% - Protein
- 30% - Healthy Fats
- 20% - Carbohydrates
- 20% - Vitamins and Minerals

If you don't want to spend your time perusing the nutritional facts of each dog food brand to ensure that you are following the correct proportions, don't worry, because in the next section you will find specific brands that are handpicked and deemed the best foods by breeders for our precious Frenchies.

High-Quality Dog Food Brands for your French Bulldog

Shopping for dog food can be overwhelming for some dog owners simply because there are so many different options to choose from and so many things to consider. Lucky for you this section will make your life easier by providing the top brand recommendations of breeders for your French Bulldog. All you have to do now is search for stores that sell these brands or order on Amazon.

These are ranked according to favorites:

1. FROMM Game Bird Recipe Dog Food (Grain-Free) The extensive analysis taken from their official website presents sufficient basis for earning the number one spot:

GENERAL			
	As-Is Basis (%)	Dry Matter Basis (%)	Dry Matter Basis (grams/100 kcal)
Protein	29.65	31.64	7.81
Fat	18.29	19.52	4.82
Fiber	3.39	3.62	0.89
Moisture	6.28		
Ash	6.48	6.91	1.71
Carbohydrates	35.91	38.32	9.46
Omega 6 Fatty Acids	3.49	3.72	0.92
Omega 3 Fatty Acids	0.79	0.84	0.21
Taurine	0.12	0.12	0.03
	As-Is Basis (CFU/g)		
Total Microorganisms	220,264 Min.		
MINERALS			
	As-Is Basis (%)	Dry Matter Basis (%)	Dry Matter Basis (grams/100 kcal)

Calcium	1.19	1.27	0.31
Phosphorus	0.95	1.01	0.25
Sodium	0.36	0.38	0.09
Potassium	0.81	0.86	0.21
Magnesium	0.15	0.16	0.04
	As-Is Basis (mg/kg)	Dry Matter Basis (mg/kg)	Dry Matter Basis (mg/100 kcal)
Zinc	198	211.27	5.22
Iron	219	233.67	5.77
Manganese	72	76.82	1.9
Copper	21	22.41	0.55
Cobalt	0.4	0.43	0.01
Iodine	1.68	1.79	0.04
Selenium	0.47	0.5	0.01
VITAMINS			
	As-Is Basis (IU/kg)	Dry Matter Basis (IU/kg)	Dry Matter Basis (IU/100 kcal)
Vitamin A	21,233	22,655.78	559.6
Vitamin D	1,517	1,618.65	39.98
Vitamin E	210	224.07	5.53
	As-Is Basis (mg/kg)	Dry Matter Basis (mg/kg)	Dry Matter Basis (mg/100 kcal)
Vitamin B12	0.12	0.12	0.003
Choline Chloride	2,706	2,887.32	71.32
Niacin	99	105.63	2.61
Pantothenic Acid	30	32.01	0.79
Vitamin C (Ascorbic Acid)	44	47.3	1.17
Riboflavin	8	8.54	0.21
Thiamine	10	10.67	0.26
Pyridoxine	4.9	5.23	0.13
Folic Acid	1.8	1.92	0.05
Biotin	0.35	0.37	0.01

2. Taste of the Wild – Exotic Formulations
   A premium choice that is more affordable than FROMM. It is 100% natural with a wide variety of exotic meats that are surely agreeable to your Frenchie's taste buds.

3. Grandma Lucy's Freeze-Dried Dog Food
   First-class, wet dog food made out of all safe ingredients that is practical because a bag can last

for as long as a month and a half. Recommended only for puppies because adult dogs need hard food for dental care.

4. Addiction's Wild Kangaroo & Apple Dog Food
   This is the ideal choice: affordable, easy to find, tasty, simple yet fun.

5. Natural Balance Premium Limited Ingredients Dog Food
   The least expensive brand but that doesn't diminish the high-quality of this everyday dog food that is great for French Bulldogs.

6. Wellness CORE Natural Dog Food
   Made for French Bulldogs, this brand offers a whole and balanced diet. It's simple and organic.

7. Earthborn Holistic Coastal Catch Grain-Free Dry Dog Food
   Like the previous two brands, this is another basic but complete option. It was made for the sensitive tummies of French Bulldogs that decreases flatulence.

| 1.FROMM | 2.Taste of the Wild | 3.Grandma Lucy's | 4.Addiction's |

5.Natural Balance   6.CORE Wellness   7.Earthborn

Tips for Feeding Your French Bulldog

Just like people, dogs have different personalities. French Bulldogs could be active or lazy so their feeding depends on which category they fall under. This breed is prone to obesity and it is very important that you do not permit this to happen because there's a big chance it will lead to more serious health complications.

Some Frenchies are overly enthusiastic during mealtimes and they tend to eat too fast or too much so it would be a good idea to watch as he eats and make sure he doesn't gobble up his food too fast. The trick is to control the amount by giving him small portions, and then wait a while before giving again. This is important because eating rapidly may cause your dog's stomach to flip, which is a very serious and sometimes fatal medical condition known as Gastric dilation and volvulus. Another way to avoid this is by feeding your pet four times spread out through the day. That's the ideal method for feeding but if you don't have the time for it, twice or thrice a day should be fine as long as you implement the supervision technique discussed earlier.

Puppies need a total 1.5 cups of dog food in one day that should be split according to his meal schedule. Mature dogs need an average total of 2-3 cups a day, also split according to his meal schedule.

Dangerous Foods to Avoid

It might be tempting to give in to your dog when he is begging at the table, but certain "people foods" can actually be toxic for your dog. As a general rule, you should never feed your dog anything unless you are 100% sure that it is safe. Below you will find a list of foods that can be toxic to dogs and should therefore be avoided:

- Alcohol
- Apple seeds
- Avocado
- Cherry pits

- Chocolate
- Coffee
- Garlic
- Grapes/raisins
- Hops
- Macadamia nuts
- Mold
- Mushrooms
- Mustard seeds
- Onions/leeks
- Peach pits
- Potato leaves/stems
- Rhubarb leaves
- Tea
- Tomato leaves/stems
- Walnuts
- Xylitol
- Yeast dough

If your Frenchie eats any of these foods, contact the Pet Poison Control hotline right away at (888) 426 – 4435.

Chapter Six: Training Your French Bulldog

Training dogs is like raising children. Both are difficult and will definitely test your patience at times. So much more so for this breed because they are intrinsically hard headed and disobedient. Frenchies are so adorable and irresistible that you'll often be tempted to just let them get away with the offense they've committed. If you're inherently a spoiler and you don't mind having to put up with recurring misbehaviors, then by all means, indulge them. But if you want a well-behaved dog, training is a must. In this chapter you will be taught how to housebreak and socialize your puppy. Tips for training and teaching tricks are also included in this section.

Socializing Your New French Bulldog Puppy

The first three months of life is when your puppy will be the most impressionable. This is when you need to socialize him because the experiences he has as a puppy will shape the way he interacts with the world as an adult. French Bulldogs are usually social creatures but if you don't properly socialize them then they could grow up to be a mal-adjusted adult who fears new experiences. Fortunately, socialization is very simple – all you have to do is make sure that your puppy has plenty of new experiences. <u>Below you will find a list of things you should expose your puppy to for properly socialization</u>:

- Introduce your puppy to friends in the comfort of your own home.

- Invite friends with dogs or puppies to come meet your Frenchie (make sure everyone is vaccinated).

- Expose your puppy to people of different sizes, shapes, gender, and skin color.

- Introduce your puppy to children of different ages – just make sure they know how to handle the puppy safely.

- Take your puppy with you in the car when you run errands.

- Walk your puppy in as many places as possible so he is exposed to different surfaces and surroundings.

- Expose your puppy to water from hoses, sprinklers, showers, etc. Be sure to have control over your puppy when introducing him to bodies of water that could drown him.

- Make sure your puppy experiences loud noises such as fireworks, cars backfiring, loud music, thunder, etc.

- Introduce your puppy to various appliances and tools such as blenders, lawn mowers, vacuums, etc.

- Walk your puppy with different types of harnesses and leashes.

- Once he is old enough, take your puppy to the dog park to interact with other dogs.

Positive Reinforcement for Obedience Training

Training a dog is not as difficult as many people think – it all has to do with the rewards. Think about this – if you want someone do so something for you, you probably offer them something in return. The same concept is true for dog training – if you reward your dog for performing a particular behavior then he will be more likely to repeat it in the future. This is called positive reinforcement training and it is one of the simplest yet most effective training methods you can use as a dog owner.

The key to success with dog training is two-fold. For one thing, you need to make sure that your dog understands what it is you are asking him. If he doesn't know what a command means it doesn't matter how many times you say it, he won't respond correctly. In order to teach your dog what a command means you should give it and then guide him to perform the behavior. Once he does, immediately give him a treat and praise him – the sooner you reward after identifying the desired behavior, the faster your puppy will learn.

The second key to success in dog training is consistency. While your puppy is learning basic obedience commands you need to use the same commands each and every time and you need to be consistent in rewarding him. If you maintain consistency it should only take a few repetitions for your puppy to learn what you expect of him. You can then move on to another command and alternate between them to reinforce your puppy's understanding. Just be sure to keep your training sessions short – about 5 to 10 minutes – because Frenchies have a short attention span and he will probably get bored or lose interest if you extend the time. What you can do is spread out short but frequent sessions throughout the day.

Negative Consequences for Respect Training

For a well-mannered dog who will not only follow you when you ask him to do something but who will also obey you when you ask him to stop doing unwanted actions, you need to earn his respect. Therefore, positive reinforcement is not enough training because it doesn't teach your dog to respect you. When your dog is not in the mood for a treat, they will just opt not to listen to your command. As established in this book previously, French bulldogs are a stubborn breed and when they are lead to believe that they can get away with anything they can become manipulative. As their leader, you cannot ever let them think that you are their follower or else you will have problems in getting them to listen and obey you. Hence, respect training is a must. You have to establish rules so he'll know that you're capable of being his leader. When he misbehaves, you have to tell him "no" or "stop". You have to be firm but very gentle. Never hurt, scold or yell at your Frenchie because punishment doesn't work on them. It only hurts their sensitive feelings and will cause them to sulk and mope. The good news is that French Bulldogs are generally people pleasers so when they are (gently but firmly) reprimanded, they will most likely not want to repeat the misbehavior. Remember: consistency is the key to successful training.

Crate Training - Housebreaking Your Puppy

In addition to obedience training, house training is very important for puppies. After all, you don't want to spend your dog's entire life following after him with a pooper scooper. Housebreaking a French Bulldog is no easy feat. Start saving up your patience for it. The key to housebreaking is to use your puppy's crate appropriately. When you are able to watch your puppy, keep him in the same room with you at all times and point to the litter tray in his special area once every hour or so to give him a chance to do his business. Always lead him to the litter tray and give him a command like "Go pee" so he learns what is expected of him when you take him to this area. When he succeeds at this task, be sure to reward him.

When you can't watch your puppy and overnight, you should confine him to his crate. The crate should be just large enough for your puppy to stand up, sit down, turn around and lie down in. Keeping it this size will ensure that he views the crate as his den and he will be reluctant to soil it. Just make sure that you don't keep your puppy in the crate for longer than he is physically capable of holding his bladder. Always take your puppy out before putting him in the crate and immediately after releasing him.

If you give your puppy ample opportunity to do his business in his litter tray, reward him consistently, and you keep him confined to the crate when you can't watch him, housetraining should eventually be effective. Although, the length of training is also dependent on your Frenchie's level of stubbornness. Again, consistency and positive reinforcement – not to mention patience – is crucial here so always reward and praise your puppy for doing his business in his litter trays so he learns to do it that way. If your puppy does have an accident, do not punish him because not only will he not understand – he won't associate the punishment with the crime so he will just learn to fear you instead – but also, as stated in the previous section, Frenchies are highly sensitive to scolding or negative criticism.

Teaching Tricks and Playing Games

A worthwhile way of bonding and spending quality time with your Frenchie is to incorporate play time with teaching tricks that is sure to be filled with a lot of fun and enjoyment. Games are also the ideal exercise for your Frenchie because it is less tiring and safer. When teaching tricks, only positive reinforcement should be applied. Never punish your dog for not being able to do the trick.

Fetch– Teaching your dog how to fetch is probably the most useful trick for him to learn. You'll get to teach him words, when you're lazy to get something he could get it for you, and it's an enjoyable game for him to play which serves as his daily exercise. You should start with items that will excite him like a ball, a chew toy or a bone. Make sure to properly and repeatedly label the item you are asking him to retrieve before throwing it and once he returns it, give him a reward. When his vocabulary expands, you can start making a game out of it by asking him to identify the item among a lot of other objects in the same place. Whenever he gets it right, it would be a good idea to increase the prize for motivation.

Hide and Seek – A spin-off on fetch, use the words and objects he already knows but instead of asking him to fetch it, teach him how to hide it and how to look for it. Frenchies will love this game because they are fond of hiding things and unearthing them later on. Reward him for each hidden and found object.

Go to – This is also a good trick for discipline that could be used for teaching him how to go to bed or to his litter trays to relieve his bladder or bowels. Much like the command fetch, you only have to point to the place and properly and repeatedly identify it. When he gets it right, give a reward.

Chapter Seven: Grooming Your French Bulldog Properly

Grooming is probably the only low-maintenance aspect of owning a French Bulldog. Because of their short coats, grooming tasks are easier and less time-consuming compared to dogs with long hair or fur. Again, depending on your dog's personality, he may be well-behaved or he may be fussy during grooming time which will directly affect your disposition on the task. No matter what the outcome is, this duty is inescapable and even if you try to delay or procrastinate, inevitably, nature will call upon you. This chapter is dedicated to teaching you how to groom your Frenchie properly.

Recommended Tools to Have on Hand

Since it would be a waste of money to bring your dog to a professional groomer, you will need certain tools and supplies for grooming your Frenchie at home. <u>You will find a list of several recommended grooming tools and supplies below</u>:

- Rubber hound glove or soft bristle brush
- Organic Oatmeal dog shampoo
- Moisturizer or lotion for dogs
- Petroleum jelly
- Baby powder
- Dry cloth
- Any small toothbrush
- Desitin (brand of diaper rash ointment)
- Nail clippers
- Dog-friendly ear cleaning solution
- Dog toothbrush
- Dog-friendly toothpaste
- Anti-bacterial wet wipes for babies (mild) *optional

Tips for Bathing and Grooming French Bulldogs

French Bulldogs generally like to keep themselves clean. They are not the kind of dogs that like to roll around in mud or any other activity that gets them dirty. So baths are only necessary when they start giving off doggy odor which is usually a week apart. Use only mild organic Oatmeal shampoo because that is the recommended kind suitable for the breed's sensitive skin. When giving your dog a bath, be extra careful not to get water in his ears and shampoo on the eyes, and give special attention to the folds and wrinkles, making sure to clean them completely. Dry your dog thoroughly, especially in the folds and wrinkles because moisture harbors bacteria that can lead to infections. Apply baby powder using any small toothbrush on the folds and wrinkles to keep them dry longer. This breed also obtains tear stains and the recommended remedy is applying Desitin on the affected areas, gently and cautiously avoiding the eyes. Brushing their coat is also a weekly chore so you can schedule it after every weekly bath so that way you won't forget. For brushing, you can use either a rubber hound glove or a soft bristle brush.

Other Grooming Tasks

In addition to brushing and bathing your French Bulldog, you also need to engage in some other grooming tasks including trimming your dog's nails, cleaning his ears, cleaning his folds and wrinkles, caring for dry skin and nose, and brushing his teeth. You will find an overview of each of these grooming tasks below:

Trimming Your Dog's Nails

Your dog's nails grow in the same way that your own nails grow so they need to be trimmed occasionally. For French Bulldogs, a monthly trim would suffice. Before you trim your dog's nails for the first time you should have your veterinarian or a professional groomer show you how to do it. A dog's nail contains a quick – the blood vessel that supplies blood to the nail – and if you cut the nail too short you could sever it. A severed quick will cause your dog pain and it will bleed profusely. The best way to avoid cutting your dog's nails too short is to just trim the sharp tip.

Cleaning Your Dog's Ears

The French Bulldog has bat ears, which is his trademark feature. If the dog's ears get wet it creates an environment that is beneficial for infection-causing bacteria. Regularly checking your dog's ears and making sure they are clean and dry is the key to preventing infections. If you have to clean your dog's ears, use a dog ear cleaning solution and squeeze a few drops into the ear canal. Then, massage the base of your dog's ears to distribute the solution then wipe it away using a clean cotton ball.

Cleaning Your French Bulldog's Folds And Wrinkles

The folds and wrinkles on your Frenchie require frequent maintenance. It would be great for your dog if you could remember and find the time to do it daily to guarantee optimal security against infections. But if not, the next best option would be to do it as the need arises. For example, your dog had a particularly wild meal time and you feel that he may have accumulated food particles in his folds and wrinkles. The last option is to do it weekly, a day longer than that is unacceptable for a standard responsible dog owner. To clean the areas, use his shampoo or (mild) anti-bacterial wet wipes for babies and dry thoroughly. Then apply baby powder with a small toothbrush to keep them dry longer.

Caring for Dry Skin and Nose

Frenchies have sensitive skin that is predisposed to forming patches of dry skin and hot spots. If dry skin occurs, apply moisturizer or lotion made especially for dogs. If hot spots appear, use Vetericyn Hot Spot Spray (a safe, non-toxic solution). Additionally, your dog's nose may become dry or brittle from time to time if not properly cared for. As a precaution, put petroleum jelly on the nose as often as needed.

Brushing Your Dog's Teeth

Many dog owners neglect their dog's dental health which is a serious mistake. You should brush your dog's teeth with a dog-friendly toothbrush and dog toothpaste to preserve his dental health. Feeing your dog dental treats and giving him hard rubber toys can also help to maintain his dental health.

Chapter Eight: Breeding French Bulldogs

It is important to understand that breeding should only be done by professional breeders who only aim to preserve and help the breed live longer by eliminating the genetic defects that cause oppressive health problems in the dogs. With this in mind and recalling that French Bulldogs have disastrous genes, breeding them is flat-out and forcibly discouraged. Your love for your dog should encompass the entire breed as well and you should only have their best interests at heart. Irresponsible breeding will most likely just cause damage to the female dog, the offspring and consequently to the entire breed. To further understand the controversy of breeding French Bulldogs, continue reading this chapter.

The Controversy on Breeding French Bulldogs

The entire process of breeding French Bulldogs is extremely difficult, from choosing healthy dogs all the way to raising the litter.

In determining whether a female and a male dog is suitable for breeding, tracing the lineage to find any hereditary disorders and a comprehensive result of official screening tests are needed in order to prove that the pair is completely healthy and safe for breeding.

Mating is often unsuccessful due to the proportions of the breed which make it hard for the male to reach the female, and the execution itself tires and overheats the male right away. As a result, most French Bulldogs are conceived through artificial insemination which is extravagantly costly.

Since hip dysplasia is very common in the breed, the female dogs only deliver their puppies through C-section which includes laborious recovery and the administration of a veterinarian. And in the event that the mother of the litter is unable to take care of her puppies, the gargantuan duty and responsibility falls on the breeder.

Now that you have a better understanding on breeding French Bulldogs, hopefully you are convinced that it is not something you would want to pursue.

Basic Dog Breeding Information

Given the controversy of breeding French Bulldogs, you would be hard-pressed to find explicit details about it as it is reserved only for the professional breeders. Subsequently, the data provided here and in the following section should not be practiced ignorantly and irresponsibly. If you are not a professional breeder, the following information should be taken merely as an education and enlightenment on breeding dogs in general and not specific to French Bulldogs unless otherwise specified.

The ASPCA recommends having your dogs neutered or spayed before the age of 6 months. For female dogs, six months is around the time the dog experiences her first heat. Heat is just another name for the estrus cycle in dogs and it generally lasts for about 14 to 21 days. The frequency of heat may vary slightly from one dog to another but it generally occurs twice a year. When your female dog goes into heat, this is when she is capable of becoming pregnant.

When breeding it is important that you wait until the female reaches sexual maturity. Your dog may be full-size by the time she reaches one year of age, but most breeders recommend waiting until she is two years old to breed her. Not only does this ensure that the dog is mature enough to physically carry and bear a litter, but it also provides enough time for any serious health problems to develop. If the dog does display signs of congenital health problems, she should not be bred for fear of passing them on. Preferably, your dog should only be bred every other year because if she conceives and gives birth consecutively within a short span of time it may cause problems in her reproductive system.

Once you've made sure that you have chosen the ideal breeding pair you can start to think about the details of heat and breeding. When a female dog goes into heat there are a few common signs you can look for. The first sign of heat is swelling of the vulva – this may be accompanied by a bloody discharge. Over the course of the heat cycle the discharge lightens in color and becomes more watery. By the 10th day of the cycle the discharge is light pink – this is when she begins to ovulate and it is when she is most fertile. This is the time to introduce her to the male dog. If she isn't receptive to the male's advances, wait a day or two before trying again.

A dog is technically capable of conceiving at any point during the heat cycle because the male's sperm can survive in her reproductive tract for up to 5 days. If you don't plan to breed your dog, you need to keep her locked away while she is in heat. A male dog can smell a female dog in heat from several miles away and an intact male dog will go to great lengths to breed. Never take a female dog in heat to the dog park and be very careful about taking her outside at all. Do not leave her unattended in your backyard because a stray dog could get in and breed with her.

If you want to breed your dog, you will need to keep track of her estrus cycle so you know when to breed her. It generally takes a few years for a dog's cycle to become regular. Keep track of your dog's cycle on a calendar so you know when to breed her. Tracking her cycle and making note of when you introduce her to the male dog will help you predict the due date for the puppies. Once you do start breeding your dog, be sure to skip at least one heat cycle between litters – ideally, you should give your dog a year to rest between litters.

Breeding Tips and Raising Puppies

After the male dog fertilizes the egg inside the female's body, the female will go through the gestation period during which the puppies start to develop inside her womb. The gestation period for French Bulldogs lasts for anywhere from 60 to 63 days with the average being 61. However, you won't be able to actually tell that your dog is pregnant until after the third week. By the 25th day of pregnancy it is safe for a vet to perform an ultrasound and by day 28 he should be able to feel the puppies by palpating the female's abdomen. At the six week mark an x-ray can be performed to check the size of the litter. The average litter size for French Bulldogs is between 3 and 5 puppies.

While the puppies are growing inside your female dog's belly you need to take careful care of her. You don't need to feed your dog any extra until the fourth or fifth week of pregnancy when she really starts to gain weight. Make sure to provide your dog with a healthy diet and keep up with regular vet appointments to make sure the pregnancy is progressing well. Once you reach the fifth week of pregnancy you can increase your dog's daily rations in proportion to her weight gain.

After eight weeks of gestation you should start to get ready for your dog to give birth – in dogs, this is called whelping. You should have a mode of transportation ready and pack a bag that contains everything that she will and might need. Be prepared to take off for the veterinary clinic under time pressure.

When your dog is ready to give birth her internal temperature will decrease slightly. If you want to predict when the puppies will be born you can start taking her internal temperature once a day during the last week of gestation. When the dog's body temperature drops from 100°F to 102°F (37.7°C to 38.8°C to about 98°F (36.6°C), labor is likely to begin very soon. At this point your dog will display obvious signs of discomfort such as pacing, panting, or changing positions. Just let her do her own thing but keep an eye on her in case of complications.

During the early stages of labor, your dog will experience contractions about 10 minutes apart. If she has contractions for more than 2 hours without giving birth, bring her to the vet immediately. Whelping through C-section is entirely different from normal delivery. It is very unpredictable and it's a case-to-case basis.

It is essential that the puppies start nursing as soon as possible after whelping so that they get the colostrum. The colostrum is the first milk a mother produces and it is loaded with nutrients as well as antibodies that will protect the puppies while their own immune systems continue developing. The puppies will generally start nursing on their own or the mother will encourage them. After the puppies nurse for a little while you should make sure that your mother dog eats something as well.

The newborn French Bulldog puppies only weigh about 10-14 ounces and they will continue growing over the next several months until they zone in on their adult size. It is a good idea to weigh the puppies once a week or so to make sure they are growing at a healthy rate. When puppies are born they will have some very fine hair but it isn't enough to keep them warm – your mother dog will help with that. It is also very important to place the puppies in a warm place or under a light. The puppies will be born with their eyes and ears closed but they will start to open around 10 to 12 days following birth.

Your puppies will be heavily dependent on their mother for the first few weeks of life until they start becoming more mobile. Around 5 to 6 weeks of age you should start offering your puppies small amounts of solid food soaked in broth or water to start the weaning process. Over the next few weeks the puppies will start to nurse less and eat more solid food. Around 10 weeks of age they should be completely weaned – this is when they are ready to be separated from their mother.

Chapter Nine: Showing Your French Bulldog

One of the joys of owning a pure-breed dog is the challenge to participate in dog shows. If you're entertaining the idea, you must ask yourself if your dog is well-mannered, confident, and exceptionally trained. And then ask yourself if you have the time and patience that you need to dedicate in this endeavor. If you've answered yes to both questions and you've decided to pursue the challenge, the first thing you need to do is check if your French Bulldog has all the requirements of AKC to become a show dog. This chapter provides a summary of the standards of the AKC for a French Bulldog and how to prepare your dog for a show.

French Bulldog Breed Standard

The AKC breed standard for the French Bulldog provides guidelines for both breeding and showing. AKC-registered breeders must select dogs that adhere to the standards of the breed and all French Bulldog owners who seek to show their dogs at AKC shows must compare them to the official breed standard as well. <u>Below you will find an overview of the breed standard for the American French Bulldog breed</u>:

General Appearance and Temperament

The French Bulldog is a small, muscular and sturdy dog that appears to be intelligent because of the curious expression on the face and alert because of the perky ears and bright eyes. Well-behaved, adaptable, calm and affectionate.

Head and Neck

The head is large and square with a slightly round forehead and flat on the top between the ears. Bat ears that are wide at the base, elongating to a round tip, erect with the orifice facing front. They are situated high on the head with substantial space in between them. Round, dark colored eyes positioned low and far from ears, set wide apart, neither big or small, neither bulging or deep-set. Black, flat nose with big nostrils and a clear line between them is the center of the face where the well-defined cheeks form wrinkles above it. The muzzle is broad and deep. Thick, black lips hanging over the lower jaw on the sides that blends with the underlip. The underjaw is square and undershot. The neck is arched and thick with wrinkles at the throat.

Body and Tail

The body is short, well-rounded with tucked up belly. The chest is deep, ample and broad. The tail has a thick base and a fine tip and is carried low. It's short and either straight or screwed.

Legs and Feet

The forequarters are straight, stout, burly and set wide apart. The hindquarters are powerful and well-muscled, and longer than the forequarters. The hocks are well let down. Feet are medium-sized, compact and firmly set. Hindfeet are slightly bigger than forefeet. Toes are compact but evenly split with high knuckles and stubby nails. Dewclaws may be removed.

Coat and Texture

The coat is short and smooth. Skin is soft and wrinkled at the head and shoulders.

Color

Brindle, fawn, white, brindle and white and any color that isn't included in the disqualifications

Size

Should not exceed 28 pounds.

Gait

The gait should be unrestrained, well-coordinated, free and energetic.

Disqualifications

- Any alteration other than dew claws removed
- Over 28 pounds
- Nose that isn't black, unless dog is light-colored
- Solid black, black and tan, mouse, liver, black and white, white with black
- Light colored eyes, unless dog is light-colored

Preparing Your French Bulldog for Show

Once you've determined that your Frenchie is a good representation of the official breed standard, then you can think about entering him in a dog show. Dog shows occur all year-round in many different locations so check the AKC or Kennel Club website for shows in your area. Remember, the rules for each show will be different so make sure to do your research so that you and your dog are properly prepared for the show.

On the following page you will find a list of some general and specific recommendations to follow during show prep:

- Make sure that your Frenchie is properly socialized to be in an environment with many other dogs and people.

- Ensure that your dog is completely housetrained and able to hold his bladder for at least several hours.

- Solidify your dog's grasp of basic obedience – he should listen and follow basic commands.

- Do some research to learn the requirements for specific shows before you choose one – make sure your dog meets all the requirements for registration.

- Make sure that your dog is caught up on his vaccinations (especially Bordetella since he will be around other dogs) and have your vet clear his overall health for show.

- Have your dog groomed about a week before the show and then take the necessary steps to keep his coat clean and in good condition.

- Teach your Frenchie to stand squarely with his head held high and how to slightly trot – not walk or run.

In addition to making sure that your French Bulldog meets the requirements for the show and is a good representation of the AKC breed standard, you should also pack a bag of supplies that you will need on the day of show. Below you will find a list of helpful things to include in your dog show supply pack:

- Registration information
- Dog crate or exercise pen
- Grooming table and grooming supplies
- Food and treats
- Food and water bowls
- Trash bags
- Medication (if needed)
- Change of clothes
- Food/water for self
- Paper towels or rags
- Toys for the dog

If you want to show your dog but you don't want to jump immediately into an AKC show, you may be able to find some local dog shows in your area. Local shows may be put on by a branch of a national French Bulldog breed club and they can be a great place to learn and to connect with other Frenchie owners.

Chapter Ten: Keeping Your Dog Healthy

We all want our dogs to live the longest life possible with the most minimal discomfort achievable. With that said, health care should never be neglected and taken for granted, especially for our beloved French Bulldog breed. Another challenge of owning this breed is keeping him healthy because unfortunately, this breed is more prone to getting sick than most other breeds. As previously mentioned in Chapter 2, they are amongst the most expensive in terms of medical costs. Their health care is high-maintenance so before you make your final decision on getting one, please make sure that you are ready to deal with the potential stress—and in the worst case possible—crippling heartbreak that these illnesses could cause. Do your dog a favor and find out the best ways to ensure his long and healthy life in this chapter.

Common Health Problems Affecting French Bulldogs

The most problematic flaw of French Bulldogs is their health. It is easier to deal with stubbornness and the difficulty of training rather than having to witness your dog suffering from illnesses and other conditions that could sometimes lead to fatalities.

Prevention is better than cure so while it's still early, take the time to learn about the common health afflictions of the breed so that you will be somewhat prepared and knowledgeable in the event that any of them occurs. In this section, you will receive an orientation about the common health problems that could affect your bulldog.

Some of the common conditions affecting French Bulldogs include:

- Allergies
- Hip dyplasia
- Brachycephalic Syndrome
- Elongated Soft Palate
- Heat Stroke
- Hemivertebra
- Patellar Luxation
- Intervertebral Disc Disease
- Von Willebrand's Disease

Allergies

Just like humans, dogs can develop allergic reactions to a number of different things. An allergy develops when the dog's immune system identifies a substance as pathogenic, or dangerous, and it launches an attack. The three main types of allergens can be inhaled, ingested, or taken into the body through skin contact. Dogs can develop allergies at any time and some breeds are more prone to allergies than others such as Cocker Spaniels, Terriers, Retrievers, Setters, and brachycephalic breeds like Pugs and Bulldogs.

Common symptoms of allergies in dogs include red or itchy skin, runny eyes, increased scratching, ear infections, sneezing, vomiting, diarrhea, and swollen paws. Some common allergens for dogs include smoke, pollen, mold, dust, dander, feathers, fleas, medications, cleaning products, certain fabrics, and certain foods. Surprisingly, food allergies tend to produce skin-related symptoms like itching and scratching rather than digestive symptoms. Chronic ear infections are also a common sign of food allergies in dogs. The best treatment for allergies is avoiding contact with the allergen. For some environmental allergens, your vet might prescribe antihistamines or your vet might give your dog an injection to protect him.

Hip Dysplasia

This condition is genetic that is developed through external factors such as over-exercising at a young age and obesity. Basically, this condition is a malformation of the hip sockets that will later on cause arthritis. It is a painful condition that will affect your dog's gait. For hereditary conditions, there are no preventions. The only thing you can do is slow down the progression of the disease. You can do this by monitoring your dog's exercise and physical activities and make sure that he only gets the right amount without potentially damaging the joints (e.g. refrain your dog from jumping), watching his diet; don't overfeed him to prevent obesity and take care to give him a balanced amount of calcium.To save yourself the trouble, make sure your breeder presents you with proof that the parents of your dog have been screened for Hip Dysplasia and results yield negative. For treatment, there are different kinds of surgeries available depending on the case but the cost is appalling. Instead, you can settle for massage and physical therapy.

Brachycephalic Syndrome

This syndrome typically occurs in dogs with flat faces and short noses, or elongated soft palates. It is a severe respiratory disorder that could be fatal if the dog is unable to keep up with the release of carbon dioxide in exchange for oxygen. This is caused by obstructed airways that are subject to more distress when the dog is over-exercised, stressed or left too long in the heat. Symptoms include labored breathing, vomiting, choking, snoring, prolonged and frequent panting. If your dog exhibits any of these signs, take him to the vet as soon as possible. A lot of bulldogs die because this condition isn't taken too seriously and is commonly thought as just traits that come with the breed. Home remedies include a balanced healthy diet, staying away from heat, too much exercise, and using a harness instead of a collar so that the trachea isn't constricted. Swimming and flying on planes are also strictly prohibited since the risk for instant death is extremely high. Treatment depends on the severity of the condition (e.g. cool temperatures, sedatives, intubation, surgery, etc.).

Elongated Soft Palate

The Elongated Soft Palate abnormality is one of the causes of Brachycephalic Syndrome in which the elongated soft palate blocks the airway and makes breathing difficult for the dog. This is a congenital defect, thus, it cannot be prevented but it can be corrected through surgery. The same symptoms, treatments and home remedies for Brachycephalic Syndrome apply to this condition as well.

Heat Stroke

French Bulldogs are not built to endure heat, warm and humid weather. Because of their compressed airways, they have difficulty regulating their body temperature which could lead to a fatal heat stroke. It is important to keep your Frenchie in cool temperatures and to make sure that he has access to water at all times.

Hemivertebrae

This is an inborn deformity of one or more back bones that is usually shaped like a wedge or triangle causing the spine to twist. This condition varies in severity and in mild cases signs are generally unseen. Meanwhile, in the worst cases, compression of the spinal cord can lead to pain, weakness and paralysis. Being a congenital defect, there is no known cause or prevention aside from responsible breeding. Decompression surgery is an available treatment.

Patellar Luxation

Patellar Luxation is just a fancy (scientific) name for Kneecap Dislocation. Though it's a birth defect, the misalignment doesn't come about until they're grown adults. This is common in small breed dogs and it can be seen when a dog has an uneven and unusual gait. Like hip dysplasia, this is a joint disorder which can also lead to arthritis. The severity ranges from mild to serious. In mild cases, the dislocation happens intermittently and the kneecap naturally realigns itself. In the most serious cases, surgery is required.

Intervertebral Disc Disease (IDD)

IDD is the occurrence of a rupturing or herniating disc in the spine which then thrusts into the spinal cord. This thrusting movement disables the nerve transmissions to mobilize along the spinal cord which may cause paralysis. IDD can be caused by trauma, age, or simply from a sudden jolt like a bad fall or a miscalculated jump. This disease is very painful and may render your dog weak and unwilling to move. Medical treatment typically involves nonsteroidal anti-inflammatory drugs (NSAIDS) that are specifically manufactured for dogs and keeping the dog in confinement where he will be unable to make big movements. Surgery for extreme cases can only be administered within the first day of the injury. Recovery and healing period after the surgery may take a few months and will also require both medical treatments.

Von Willebrand's Disease

This is a blood disorder that afflicts a lot of dog breeds, mainly involving the dysfunction of blood clotting. A dog suffering from this disease will exhibit signs of excessive and abnormal bleeding. Symptoms include nose bleeds, bleeding gums, persistent bleeding during and after surgery, and extended bleeding during in-heat periods or after giving birth. Sometimes blood is found in bowel wastes. This disease is normally detected between the ages of 3 and 5. The bad news is that this disease is incurable. The good news is that there are existing treatments to help your dog cope with the illness such as searing and stitching wounds and blood transfusions before undergoing surgical procedures.

Preventing Illness with Vaccinations

The best way to keep your bulldog healthy is to provide him with a nutritious and balanced diet. You also need to ensure that he gets proper veterinary care, and that includes routine vaccinations. Vaccinations will not protect your dog against nutritional deficiencies or inherited conditions, but they can help to protect him from certain communicable diseases like rabies, distemper, and parvovirus.

The vaccinations your Frenchie needs may vary depending where you live since certain regions have a higher risk for certain diseases. Your vet will know which vaccinations your dog needs and when he needs them, but the vaccination schedule below will help you to keep track of when your dog needs to see the vet.

To give you an idea what kind of vaccinations your puppy will need, consult the vaccination schedule below:

Vaccination Schedule for Dogs**			
Vaccine	**Doses**	**Age**	**Booster**
Rabies	1	12 weeks	annual
Distemper	3	6-16 weeks	3 years
Parvovirus	3	6-16 weeks	3 years
Adenovirus	3	6-16 weeks	3 years
Parainfluenza	3	6 weeks, 12-14 weeks	3 years
Bordetella	1	6 weeks	annual
Lyme Disease	2	9, 13-14 weeks	annual
Leptospirosis	2	12 and 16 weeks	annual
Canine Influenza	2	6-8, 8-12 weeks	annual

** Keep in mind that vaccine requirements may vary from one region to another. Only your vet will be able to tell you which vaccines are most important for the region where you live.

French Bulldog Care Sheet

In reading this book, you have received a combination of valuable facts, instructions and advice that has given you a comprehensive understanding of caring for a French Bulldog as a pet. If you have decided to get your own Frenchie, you will still find this book useful as you spend your days living with your dog. But rather than flipping through the entire book, you can use this care sheet as your quick reference for the most basic information you might want to recall and review. This care sheet is a summary of all the useful things that a Frenchie owner needs.

1.) Basic French Bulldog Information

Pedigree: exact origin unknown, debatable between England and France

AKC Group: Companion, Non-sporting

Breed Size: small but muscular

Height: average 12 inches

Weight: 22 – 28 pounds

Coat Length: short

Coat Texture: fine and smooth

Shedding: minimal

Color: brindle, fawn, white, brindle and white, black, mouse, cream, chocolate, gray

Eyes: dark in color, lighter in light colored coats – no white showing when looking forward

Nose: black

Ears: bat ears

Tail: short, hung low, straight or screwed

Temperament: clownish, affectionate, well-behaved, easygoing, playful, alert

Strangers: generally friendly to everyone

Children: generally good with children, but (like all dogs) should be supervised around young and small children

Other Dogs: generally good with other dogs and other animals if properly trained and socialized

Training: difficult due to short attention span and stubbornness

Exercise Needs: minimal exercise needed, daily 15-minute walks are sufficient

Health Conditions: respiratory disorders, joint diseases, blood disease, spinal disorders

Lifespan: 8 to 14 years

Nickname: Frenchie

2.) Habitat Requirements

Recommended Accessories: crate, dog bed, fences/gates, food/water dishes, toys, leash, harness, grooming supplies

Harness: sized by weight

Grooming Supplies: organic oatmeal shampoo for dogs, rubber hound glove or soft bristle brush, baby powder

Grooming Frequency: brush and bathe weekly

Energy Level: moderate – ranges from being couch potatoes to being active and playful

Exercise Requirements: 15 minute daily walk – no more, no less

Crate: highly recommended

Crate Size: just large enough for dog to lie down and turn around comfortably

Crate Extras: orthopedic bed

Toys: start with an assortment, see what the dog likes; include some mentally stimulating toys

Exercise Ideas: walks or indoor games

Food/Water bowls: stainless steel or ceramic bowls, clean daily

3.) Nutritional Needs

Nutritional Needs: water, protein, carbohydrate, fats, vitamins, minerals

Restrictions: grains, soy, corn

Calorie Needs: varies by age, weight, and activity level

Amount to Feed (puppy): 1.5-2 cups a day

Amount to Feed (adult): 2-3 cups a day

Feeding Frequency: two to four meals daily

Important Ingredients: fresh animal protein (chicken, beef, lamb, turkey, eggs), digestible carbohydrates, animal fats

Important Minerals: calcium, phosphorus, potassium, magnesium, iron, copper and manganese

Important Vitamins: Vitamin A, Vitamin A, Vitamin B-12, Vitamin D, Vitamin C

Dog Food Brands to choose from: FROMM Game Bird Recipe Dog Food (Grain-Free), Taste of the Wild – Exotic Formulations, Grandma Lucy's Freeze-Dried Dog Food, Addiction's Wild Kangaroo & Apple Dog Food, Natural Balance Premium Limited Ingredients Dog Food, Wellness CORE Natural Dog Food, Earthborn Holistic Coastal Catch Grain-Free Dry Dog Food

4.) Breeding Information

Age of First Heat: around 6 months (or earlier)

Heat (Estrus) Cycle: 14 to 21 days

Frequency: twice a year, every 6 to 7 months

Breeding Age: at least 2 years old, no more than 8

Breeding Pair: both healthy

Time Between Litters: at least one heat cycle, ideally one year

Greatest Fertility: 11 to 15 days into the cycle

Gestation Period: 60 to 63 days, average 61 days

Pregnancy Detection: possible after 21 days, best to wait 28 days before exam

Feeding Pregnant Dogs: maintain normal diet until week 5 or 6 then slightly increase rations

Signs of Labor: body temperature drops below normal 100° to 102°F (37.7° to 38.8°C), may be as low as 98°F (36.6°C); dog begins nesting in a dark, quiet place

Contractions: period of 10 minutes in waves of 3 to 5 followed by a period of rest

Whelping: C-section

Puppies: born with eyes and ears closed; eyes open at 10-12 days, teeth develop at 4-5 weeks

Litter Size: 3 to 5 puppies

Size at Birth: about 10-14 ounces

Weaning: start offering puppy food soaked in water at 6 weeks; fully weaned by 10 weeks

Socialization: start as early as possible to prevent puppies from being nervous as an adult

5.) First Aid Kit

In case of an emergency, all dog owners should have a first aid kit which consists of the following:

- Magnifying glass
- Scissors
- Tweezers
- Nail clippers and metal nail file
- Styptic powder
- Penlight
- Eye dropper or oral syringe
- Cotton swabs
- Cotton balls
- Clean towels – cloth and paper
- Rectal thermometer
- Lubricant such as mineral oil or Petroleum Jelly
- Disposable gloves
- Bitter Apple or other product to discourage chewing
- Pet carrier
- 2 Towels or blankets to use as a stretcher and insulator
- Cold packs and heat packs (wrap in towel before

using)

- Wound disinfectant such as Betadine or Nolvasan
- Triple antibiotic ointment for skin
- Antibiotic ophthalmic ointment for eyes,

e.g.,Terramycin

- Eye wash solution
- Sterile saline
- Antidiarrheal medicine
- Antihistamine for allergic reactions
- Cortisone spray to aid in itch relief
- Ear cleaning solution
- Hydrogen peroxide
- Activated charcoal to absorb ingested poisons
- Square gauze of various sizes – some sterile
- Non-stick pads
- First aid tape – both paper and adhesive types
- Bandage rolls – gauze and Vetwrap
- Band-Aids

Important Note: Before administering first aid on your dog, be sure to consult your veterinarian and ask about the important data you need.

Index

C

D

E

F

G

H

S

T

V

W

References

"11 Charming Facts About Bulldogs." Mental Floss. <http://mentalfloss.com/article/63568/11-charming-facts-about-french-bulldogs>

"French Bulldog" VetStreet.

<http://www.vetstreet.com/dogs/french-bulldog>

"French Bulldog." Dog Time.

<http://dogtime.com/dog-breeds/french-bulldog>

"French Bulldog Temperament - What's Good About 'Em What's Bad About Them" Your Pure Bred Puppy."

<http://www.yourpurebredpuppy.com/reviews/frenchbulldogs.html>

"French Bulldog." PetBreeds.

<http://dogs.petbreeds.com/l/68/French-Bulldog>

"AKC French Bulldogs Breed Standards." AKC.
<http://images.akc.org/pdf/breeds/standards/FrenchBulldo
g.pdf?_ga=1.61428524.1413678337.1464122831>

"French Bulldog." Dog Breed Info Center.
<http://www.dogbreedinfo.com/frenchbulldog.htm>

"French Bulldog." Wikipedia.
<https://en.wikipedia.org/wiki/French_Bulldog>

"French Bulldog Breed." Pet Wave.
<http://www.petwave.com/Dogs/Breeds/French-
Bulldog.aspx>

"Grooming French Bulldogs." Your French Bulldog
Health. <http://yourfrenchbulldoghealth.com/grooming-
french-bulldogs/>

"French Bulldog Breeding – Can I Do It?" All About
Frenchies.
<http://allaboutfrenchies.com/french-bulldog-breeding/>

"Best Food For French Bulldogs." All About Frenchies. <http://allaboutfrenchies.com/best-food-for-french-bulldogs/>

"Everything You Need For Your New French Bulldog Puppy." All About Frenchies. <http://allaboutfrenchies.com/french-bulldog-puppy/>

Photo Credits

Introduction Photo by OLGA1976 via Pixabay.

<https://pixabay.com/en/dog-pets-french-bulldog-1111650/>

Chapter 1 Photo by TIMHWOODCOCK via Pixabay.

<https://pixabay.com/en/french-bulldog-dog-canine-pet-1104365/>

Breed History Photo by JLVALENTEviaPixabay.

<https://pixabay.com/en/dog-french-bulldog-bulldog-pet-678020/>

Chapter 2 Photo by KRIKA_BE0 via Pixabay.

<https://pixabay.com/en/bulldog-puppy-animal-funny-doggy-648583/>

Chapter 3 Photo by MAKUNIN via Pixabay.

<https://pixabay.com/en/dog-animals-pets-bulldog-115078/>

How to choose a reputable dog breeder Photo by GLADY via Pixabay.

<https://pixabay.com/en/french-bulldog-dog-puppy-pet-277255/>

Puppy-proofing Photo by MAKUNIN viaPixabay.
<https://pixabay.com/en/french-bulldog-dog-puppy-pet-115072/>

Chapter 4 Photo by INSPIREDIMAGES via Pixabay.
<https://pixabay.com/en/bulldog-puppy-animal-dog-pet-1230083/>

Habitat and Exercise Requirements Photo by KRIKA_BE0 via Pixabay.
<https://pixabay.com/en/bulldog-french-dog-puppy-pet-648579/>

Chapter 5 Photo by ELVISCLOOTH via Pixabay.
<https://pixabay.com/en/bulldog-beach-coast-domburg-french-1381168/>

Tips for feeding Photo by YOTYLER via Pixabay.
<https://pixabay.com/en/dog-french-bulldog-black-and-white-656123/>

Food Brands Photos by Amazon via AllAboutFrenchies.<http://allaboutfrenchies.com/best-food-for-french-bulldogs/>

Chapter 6 Photo by WINSKER via Pixabay.
<https://pixabay.com/en/dog-bulldog-french-bulldog-pet-270564/>

Positive Reinforcement Photo by GK0914JP via Pixabay.
<https://pixabay.com/en/dog-cute-french-bulldog-1016918/>

Crate Training Photo by WINSKER via Pixabay.
<https://pixabay.com/en/puppy-cute-close-up-sleepy-486744/>

Chapter 7 Photo by PAROCA71 via Pixabay.
<https://pixabay.com/en/french-bulldog-dog-sea-pet-cute-1353385/>

Chapter 8 Photo by MAKUNIN via Pixabay.
<https://pixabay.com/en/dog-dogs-bulldog-french-bulldog-126164/>

Breeding Tips and Raising Puppies Photo by MAKUNIN via Pixabay.
<https://pixabay.com/en/dog-dogs-bulldog-french-bulldog-126164/>

Chapter 9 Photo by 825545 via Pixabay.
<https://pixabay.com/en/french-bulldog-puppy-tunnel-meadow-665152/>

Preparing your French Bulldog for Show Photo by 825545 via Pixabay.

<https://pixabay.com/en/french-bulldog-puppy-beagle-662818/>

Chapter 10 Photo by GK0914JP via Pixabay.

<https://pixabay.com/en/dog-cute-french-bulldog-1016920/>

Preventing Illness with Vaccinations Photo by GK0914JP via Pixabay.

<https://pixabay.com/en/dog-cute-french-bulldog-1017048/>

Care Sheet Photo by LIGHTSTARGOD via Pixabay.

<https://pixabay.com/en/dog-model-french-bulldog-view-1224267/>

Feeding Baby
Cynthia Cherry
978-1941070000

Axolotl
Lolly Brown
978-0989658430

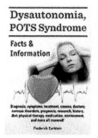

Dysautonomia, POTS
Syndrome
Frederick Earlstein
978-0989658485

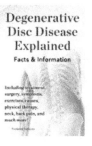

Degenerative Disc
Disease Explained
Frederick Earlstein
978-0989658485

Sinusitis, Hay Fever,
Allergic Rhinitis Explained
Frederick Earlstein
978-1941070024

Wicca
Riley Star
978-1941070130

Zombie Apocalypse
Rex Cutty
978-1941070154

Capybara
Lolly Brown
978-1941070062

Eels As Pets
Lolly Brown
978-1941070167

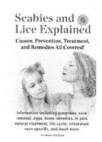

Scabies and Lice Explained
Frederick Earlstein
978-1941070017

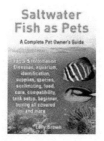

Saltwater Fish As Pets
Lolly Brown
978-0989658461

Torticollis Explained
Frederick Earlstein
978-1941070055

Kennel Cough
Lolly Brown
978-0989658409

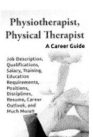

Physiotherapist, Physical
Therapist
Christopher Wright
978-0989658492

Rats, Mice, and Dormice
As Pets
Lolly Brown
978-1941070079

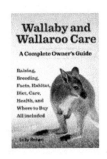

Wallaby and Wallaroo Care
Lolly Brown
978-1941070031